WINDY CITY WILD
Chicago's Natural Wonders

Photography by Robert Shaw and Jason Lindsey

Foreword by Bill Kurtis

CHICAGO REVIEW PRESS

Library of Congress Cataloging-in-Publication Data

Shaw, Robert.

 Windy City wild : Chicago's natural wonders / photography by Robert
Shaw and Jason Lindsey ; foreword by Bill Kurtis.

   p. cm.

 ISBN 1-55652-416-1

1. Chicago Region (Ill.)—Pictorial works. 2. Natural
history—Illinois—Chicago Region—Pictorial works. 3. Natural
areas—Illinois–Chicago Region—Pictorial works. I. Lindsey, Jason.
II. Title.

 F548.37 .S5 2000

 977.3'11—dc21

00-030728

Acknowledgments

We would both like to thank Curt and Linda Matthews, Cynthia Sherry, Gerilee Hundt, and everyone at
Chicago Review Press. We would also like to thank the people at Chicago Wilderness for their support and
dedication. Thank you to Bruce Boyd for writing an insightful epilogue, and to the Nature Conservancy for
their leading work in the Chicago area. We are grateful to Bill Kurtis for taking time out of his busy schedule
to write the foreword. We thank Roger Anderson and Michael Retter for their plant and avian identification
and Ron Panzer, George Derkovitz, and Bill Wengelewski for their biological expertise. We thank Wendell and
Florence Minor for their years of friendship, and especially want to thank Wendell for painting the great map
of the Chicago region for us.

Jason would like to thank John Rhoades for years of friendship, support, and encouragement. Much gratitude
goes to Scott and Jen Meyer, Jeff and Amy Tabb, and Todd and Kelly Heisler for a comfortable place to stay.

Robert would like to thank Dan and Ginny Smith, Gustav and Renate Hauser, and Greg Westray for giving
him a place to stay on many nights after campgrounds became very inconvenient. Thanks also to Jean Marie
for holding down the fort while he was away.

Jacket and interior design: Jason Lindsey
Photo editing and sequencing: Jason Lindsey and Robert Shaw
Map: Wendell Minor

First edition
Published by Chicago Review Press, Incorporated
814 North Franklin Street
Chicago, Illinois 60610
ISBN 1-55652-416-1

Printed in Italy

5 4 3 2 1

Waterfall on Rock Creek, Kankakee River State Park

Dedication

To my parents, Dan and Martha Lindsey, who continue to believe in me and encourage my passion for photographing

the natural world, and to my brother, Brent Lindsey, who inspires me with his knowledge of wildlife.

—J.L.

To my grandfather Cecil Reece Shaw, who lived and worked in Chicago for several years in the mid-1900s.

His ethic has become a part of me.

—R.S.

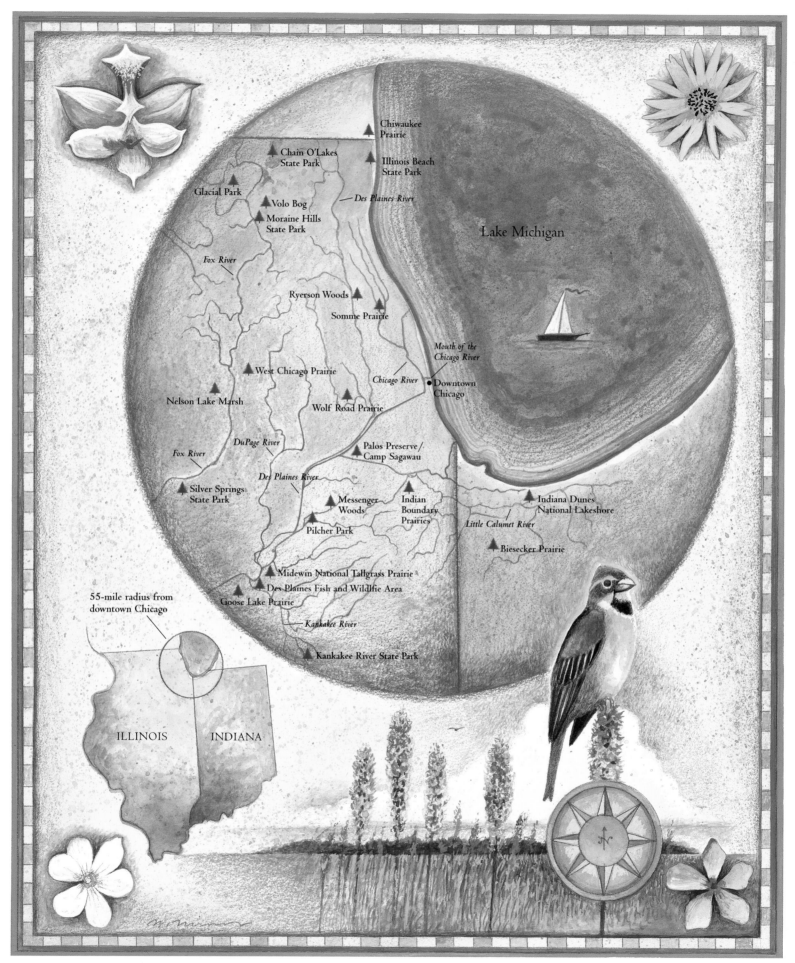

Chiwaukee Prairie

Chain O'Lakes State Park

Illinois Beach State Park

Glacial Park

Des Plaines River

Volo Bog

Moraine Hills State Park

Lake Michigan

Fox River

Ryerson Woods

Somme Prairie

Mouth of the Chicago River

West Chicago Prairie

Chicago River

Downtown Chicago

Nelson Lake Marsh

Wolf Road Prairie

DuPage River

Fox River

Palos Preserve / Camp Sagawau

Des Plaines River

Silver Springs State Park

Indiana Dunes National Lakeshore

Messenger Woods

Indian Boundary Prairies

Little Calumet River

Pilcher Park

Biesecker Prairie

Midewin National Tallgrass Prairie

Des Plaines Fish and Wildlfie Area

Goose Lake Prairie

Kankakee River

55-mile radius from downtown Chicago

Kankakee River State Park

ILLINOIS

INDIANA

Painting by Wendell Minor

6

Robert Shaw

CONTENTS

FOREWORD

The name gives us a clue: Chicago. In the language of the Potawatomi tribe it means wild onion, wild and smelly. Early voyageurs described what is now a five-mile stretch of the Chicago River, as it turns southwest past Bridgeport, as "Mud Lake," a nearly unnavigable swamp that took them two full days to cross. And that was by pulling canoes through chest-deep mud. But if you managed to slog through it, the reward was breathtaking. Rising out of the wetland was a landscape the Frenchmen had never seen before. Instead of the familiar forests there was grass, very tall grass. Rooted in deep black, peatlike soil, it swelled and crested before the wind like waves on an ocean, as far as the eye could see, until it touched the horizon. The voyageurs named it the French word for "meadow" and called it prairie.

There was something else. Occasionally, the glacial soil allowed oak trees to build council circles in the grass. Like arboreal families the "children" danced around the matriarch where acorns had sprouted on the drip line. Spreading shade and shelter like African acacia trees, the giant oaks presided over a different kind of community, the oak savanna.

Along the riverbanks and in low areas, oak and hickory trees clustered into denser woodlands. Eventually, the botanists identified the forest, prairies, and wetlands as three distinct biological systems that supported their own endemic plant communities. But the prairie was king; it was created and maintained by adequate rainfall, grazing animals such as bison, and a combination of wind and fire. This combination held back the incessant western march of trees and kept the prairie pure grass.

Just as commerce would learn that the key to Chicago's growth was location, location, location, biologists learned that Chicago's location was unique for another reason. Here at the edge of the world's greatest grassland was a very special kind of ecosystem. It erupted from the collision of the western border of the Eastern deciduous forest with the beginning of the tall-grass prairie, the southern edge of the north woods, and the remnants of Lake Michigan's southern swamps. The plant community was one of a kind.

Of course, the wave of progress rolled over these natural wonders as if they were worthless. Where there was a swamp, we felt it had to be drained and filled. Where the river ran into Lake Michigan, we reversed it and sent the waters back toward the Mississippi River. We raised streets out of the mud and paved every inch of vacant land we could find so that we could send towers toward the heavens to receive a million workers in a one-square-mile loop. The prairies were plowed under and the waving fields of big bluestem were replaced by waving fields of corn, soybeans, and wheat. Not a bad bargain—this deep rich loam fed the world.

Robert Shaw

And yet those early builders weren't completely oblivious to the beauty of open space. Drawing on the models of the great cities of the world, they set aside a collar of green space around the city's core, preserving 200,000 acres of woodlands, oak savannas, and prairie. Imagine a Seurat painting of flowing white gowns beneath the oaks, picnic baskets anchoring gingham quilts spread over the columbines, and, not far away, young men playing baseball amid coneflowers and purple liatris. It was an oasis at the end of the interurban rails. But over the years, lifestyles changed. We didn't need the natural breezes to cool off. Our entertainment kept us indoors.

As the city and farmland spread, the acres of forest and prairie preserved so carefully by early conservationists were left untouched. The prevailing attitude of conservation was "Don't touch it." "Don't burn it." "Leave it as nature intended." While laudable in its commitment, it lacked an understanding of how the system works. Prairies need occasional fires to cleanse themselves of intrusive species. The forests were savaged by buckthorn, an import from Great Britain that was used as a hedge in the northern suburbs. Its rapid growth blocked the sun from the understory, smothering the oaks and leaving the forest floor bare, devoid of the rich carpet of trilliums and jack-in-the-pulpits. The rapid-growing trees changed the hydrology to encourage even more invasion.

As the third millennium approached, biologists and ecologists discovered the dark side of a well-intended conservation effort. Nature's treasure of biodiversity so carefully preserved a century earlier was being consumed by alien intruders and would soon be replaced by a tangle of foreign plants and trees. Could it be saved?

This lush portfolio by photographers Robert Shaw and Jason Lindsey answers the question in the affirmative. It documents the reward for thousands of volunteers and over a hundred conservation organizations that searched diligently for native species and cleared the intruders away from them. They reintroduced fire into the natural equation. The result was astonishingly beautiful. Within a single season, many native plants rebounded as if they had been awakened from hibernation exclaiming, "The prairie is back!"

And so the name Chicago Wilderness was born. It describes a network task force of organizations dedicated to restoration and a new philosophy of stewardship that values our native species with the same appreciation as those Chicagoans who set out to preserve them in the first place. There is much to be done in the restoration effort. Let these pictures be our guide to what once was and what could be again.

Bill Kurtis

Blue flag iris shrouded in fog after a thunderstorm, Illinois Beach State Park

Robert Shaw

PREFACE

For many years, my photographic journeys focused on my home state, Illinois. Then I began to venture to remote regions of the United States in search of dramatic mountains, untamed rivers, and wild coastlines. I would return from places such as Yosemite, the Everglades, the Boundary Waters, and the Hawaiian Islands with images of rugged volcanic coastlines, tranquil mountain lakes, and wild rivers. But I'd be more excited about the images I had captured in Illinois. I found that my passion lies close to home—with the prairies, rivers, forests, and lakeshores of Illinois.

I then began exploring the lesser-known natural areas of Illinois and in the process discovered the astonishing biodiversity within a short drive of downtown Chicago. My passion was now sharply focused on exploring the 200,000 acres of protected land in the region. During my exploration I experienced the Oak Savanna, one of the rarest ecosystems on earth, the arctic shores of Lake Michigan, a massive sand dune reaching 190 feet into the sky, the enchanting flowers of the tall grass prairie, an ancient bog, and timeless moments with wild creatures.

Jason Lindsey

Robert Shaw and I began discussing our surprise at what we found and knew we should share our experiences. Thus, this book project officially began. We spent many months researching Chicago's natural heritage and scouting locations. We knew we had to do more than systematically document the natural areas. To open people's eyes to the natural world, we wanted to capture the allure of nature. To accomplish this, we first developed a comprehensive list of parks, ecosystems, plants, and animals. Then we spent a year and a half hiking, canoeing, kayaking, and waiting in blinds to capture thousands of images. This book presents the best of them—a dynamic portrait of the wild lands of the Windy City.

Although these pages accurately represent the Chicago region, they are not meant to glorify the metropolitan area, but to help create a new environmental awareness—an awareness of how closely we live with nature, and an awareness that we need to protect our backyard. Without that knowledge, hundreds of places like the ones pictured in this book will continue to be lost to uncontrolled and unplanned urban sprawl.

It is our hope that you will responsibly explore the natural areas of Chicago and be inspired to protect them.

Jason Lindsey

Great egret and whitetail buck, Goose Lake Prairie State Natural Area

Jason Lindsey

Cattails line the edge of Crawdad Slough, Palos Division, Cook County Forest Preserve

Cattails, Indiana Dunes National Lakeshore

PAGE 12: Winter ice on Rock Creek, Kankakee River State Park

PAGE 13: Goat's beard going to seed, Illinois Beach State Park

Fall color along the North Branch of the Chicago River, Miami Woods, Cook County Forest Preserve

Jason Lindsey

Jason Lindsey

The Illinois country is undeniably the most beautiful that is known anywhere between the mouth of the St. Lawrence River and that of the Mississippi, which are a thousand leagues apart. You begin to see its fertility at Chicago which is 140 leagues from Michillimackinac, at the end of Lake Michigan. The Chicago is a little stream only two leagues long bordered by prairies of equal dimension in width. This is a route usually taken to go to this country.

De Gannes, *Memoir*, 1695

Austrian pine trees reflecting in the Dead River, Illinois Beach State Park

Jason Lindsey

Rapids at
mouth of R
Creek, Kanka
River State P

Jason Lind

Beach grass and dunes along the shoreline of Lake Michigan at Indiana Dunes National Lakeshore

Robert Shaw

We remained five days at Kipikaoui, leaving on the 17th and after being windbound on the 18th and 19th we camped on the 20th at a place five leagues from Chikagou. We should have arrived there early on the 21st but the wind which suddenly arose on the lake compelled us to land half a league from Chikagou. We

Robert Shaw

had considerable difficulty in landing and in saving our canoes; we all had to jump into the water. One must be very careful along the lakes, and especially Lake Mixcigan, whose shores are very low, to take to the land as soon as possible when the waves rise on the lake, for the rollers become so high in so short a time that one runs the risk of breaking his canoe and of losing all it contains. Many travellers have already been wrecked there.

Jean François Buisson de St. Cosme, 1698

Icy stream in Paw Paw Woods Nature Preserve, Cook County Forest Preserve

Jason Lindsey

Sunset over a cattail marsh along the Fox River, Chain O'Lakes State Park

Jason Lindsey

Male Baltimore oriole at Chiwaukee Prairie

PAGES 24–25: Waterfall in canyon at Camp Sagawau, Sag Valley Division, Cook County Forest Preserve

Yellow-headed blackbird at the Wetlands Project, Lake County Forest Preserve

Jason Lindsey

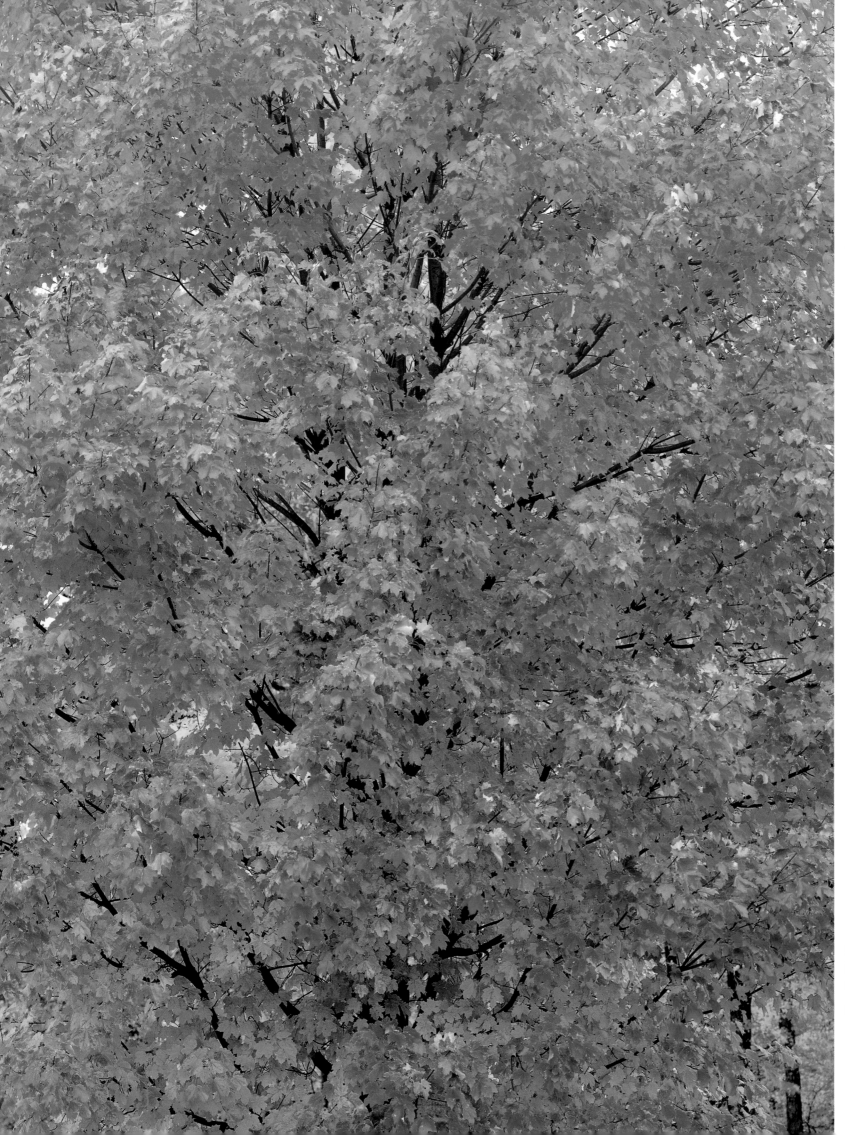

Brilliant maple,
Ryerson Woods
Conservation Area

Robert Shaw

Wild white hyacinth, Kankakee River State Park

Blazing star, early goldenrod, and flowering spurge in full bloom, Gensburg-Markham Prairie

Robert Shaw

In Chicago I first saw the beautiful prairie flowers. They were in their glory the first ten days we were there—

'The golden and flame-like flowers.'

The flame-like flower I was taught afterwards, by an Indian girl, to call 'Wickapee;' and she told me, too, that its splendors had a useful side, for it was used by the Indians as a remedy for an illness to which they were subject.

Jason Lindsey

Beside these brilliant flowers, which gemmed and gilt the grass in a sunny afternoon's drive near the blue lake, between the low oakwood and the narrow beach, stimulated, whether sensuously by the optic nerve, unused to so much gold and crimson with such tender green, or symbolically through some meaning dimly seen in the flowers, I enjoyed a sort of fairyland exultation never felt before, and the first drive amid the flowers gave me anticipation of the beauty of the prairies.

Sarah Margaret Fuller, *Summer on the Lakes*, 1843

Snowdrifts and big bluestem, Goose Lake Prairie State Natural Area

Jason Lindsey

Autumn reflections in Rock Creek, Kankakee River State Park

Robert Shaw

Water lilies cover Lake Defiance, Moraine Hills State Park

Male and female
mallards, Illinois
Beach State Park

Compass plants near sunset at Grant Creek Prairie Nature Preserve

Robert Shaw

July 7th,—I fell asleep, and when I was awakened at dawn this morning, by my companion, that I might not lose the scene, I started with surprise and delight. I was in the midst of a prairie! A world of grass and flowers stretched around me, rising and falling in gentle undulations, as if an enchanter had struck the ocean swell, and it was at rest forever. Acres of wild flowers of every hue glowed around me, and the sun arising from the earth where it touched the horizon, was 'kissing with golden face the meadows green.' What a new and wonderous world of beauty! What a magnificent sight! Those glorious ranks of flowers! Oh that you could have 'one glance at their array!' How shall I convey to you the idea

Jason Lindsey

of a prairie. I despair, for never yet hath pen brought the scene before my mind. Imagine yourself in the centre of an immense circle of velvet herbage, the sky for its boundary upon every side; the whole clothed with a radiant efflorescence of every brilliant hue. We rode thus through perfect wilderness of sweets, sending forth perfume, and animated with myriads of glittering birds and butterflies. . . .

Eliza R. Steele, *A Summer Journey in the West*, 1840

Maple leaves on the forest floor, Potawatomi Woods, Cook County Forest Preserve

Prairie dropseed, Somme Prairie Nature Preserve, Cook County Forest Preserve

Jason Lindsey

PAGES 40–41:
Ferns in autumn
along Cowles Bog
trail, Indiana Dunes
National Lakeshore

Robert Shaw

Shooting stars and
hoary puccoon in full
bloom, Chiwaukee
Prairie

Robert Shaw

Obedient plant and black-eyed Susan, Grant Creek Prairie Jason Lindsey

Goldenrod and boneset, Wolf Road Prairie Nature Preserve Jason Lindsey

Ice buildup and waves along the shoreline of Lake Michigan at North Avenue Beach, Chicago

Jason Lindsey

Peak fall color in Rock Creek Canyon, Kankakee River State Park

Large white trilliums in full bloom at Messenger Woods

Robert Shaw

Fall color in Harms Woods, Cook County Forest Preserve

Oak savanna restoration shrouded in fog, Chain O'Lakes State Park

Jason Lindsey

Beyond the young woods lies the crowing attraction of River Forest, the big woods, and presently we come to them, the finest in all the country round; untouched, first-growth timber, preserved by the dear nature-lover who has long owned the land. Here are elms no two of us can span, high and flourishing as any in New England; tall hickorys, with their swollen buds just waking up and pushing back the covers that have kept them snug and warm through the long winter; and huge gnarled oaks, trees that were never young, their sluggish blood still unstirred by the returning sun. They

Robert Shaw

are old and wise and sleep until all the spring chills and storms are over. But they do not see the young green shoots, or the white hawthorns like great bridal bouquets, or the pink crab-apples that make the woods so dainty today. They do not feel the gentle touch of the blue phlox and the violets and the buttercups against their hard dark boles, or the caressing of the sunbeams that filter through the tree tops. The oaks are old and wise and they will outlive all the rest.

Louella Chapin, *Round About Chicago*, 1907

Ox-eye daisy, West Chicago Prairie   Jason Lindsey

Rattlesnake master and goldenrod, Biesecker Prairie, Indiana   Jason Lindsey

Prairie coreopsis, goat's rue, and wild quinine in bloom, Gensburg-Markham Prairie

PAGE 50: Lizard's tail growing in a floodplain forest along the Kankakee River

PAGE 51: Sassafras trees turning color in Indiana Dunes National Lakeshore

Doe, fawn, and great egret at a prairie pothole, Goose Lake Prairie State Natural Area

Jason Lindsey

Canada geese on the Fox River, Chain O'Lakes State Park

PAGES 56–57:
Sunrise on a foggy
morning, Chain
O'Lakes State Park

Jason Lindsey

Fall colors in the
Des Plaines Division,
Cook County Forest
Preserve

Robert Shaw

Waterfall on Prairie Creek in Des Plaines Conservation Area

Rocky beach along Lake Michigan, Illinois Beach State Park

Jason Lindsey

Prairie restoration in summer display, Chain O'Lakes State Park

To the east were the moving waters as far as eye could follow.

To the west a sea of grass as far as wind might reach.

Nelson Algren, *Chicago: City on the Make*, 1951

A sandhill crane flying over the Fox River, Chain O'Lakes State Park

Robert Shaw

PAGE 62: Skunk cabbage at Black Partridge Woods, Palos Division, Cook County Forest Preserve

Robert Shaw

PAGE 63: Marsh marigolds, skunk cabbage, and bluebells in Pilcher Park

Robert Shaw

Sunrise over a wetland, Moraine Hills State Park

A pair of sandhill cranes feeding along the Fox River, Chain O'Lakes State Park

Robert Shaw

The Fox River at sunrise, Silver Springs State Park

Robert Shaw

Robert Shaw

The first day brought us through woods rich in the moccasin flower and lupine, and plains whose soft expanse was continually touched with expression by the slow moving clouds which

'Sweep over with their shadows, and beneath
The surface rolls and fluctuates to the eye;
Dark hollows seem to glide along and chase
The sunny ridges,'

to the banks of the Fox river, a sweet and graceful stream. We reached Geneva just in time to escape being drenched by a violent thunder shower, whose rise and disappearance threw expression into all the features of the scene.

Sarah Margaret Fuller, *Summer on the Lakes*, 1843

Mt. Baldy at first light, Indiana Dunes National Lakeshore

Robert Shaw

Driving winter wind in Goose Lake Prairie State Natural Area

Robert Shaw

Sawtooth sunflowers, Goose Lake Prairie State Natural Area

Jason Lindsey

Blowing prairie grass and approaching storm clouds, West Chicago Prairie

Jason Lindsey

PAGES 72–73: Giant maple, Ryerson Woods Conservation Area

Robert Shaw

Prickly pear cactus blooming at Braidwood Dunes and Savanna Nature Preserve

Robert Shaw

Oak savann
restoration sit
Morton Arboretu

Jason Linds

76

Sand reed grass along
the shoreline of Lake
Michigan at Illinois
Beach State Park

Robert Shaw

TOP: A ring-billed gull in flight over Lake Michigan   ABOVE: A feather riding the tide on the shores of Lake Michigan

Pale purple coneflowers, butterfly weed, and leadplant in a prairie restoration, Glacial Park, McHenry County Conservation District

I am highly Pleased with Michigan but I am Delighted with Illinois. Mr. Stuarts account I think is not exagerated. The first view of a Michigan Prairie is Delightfull after Passing the oak openings & thick forest, but the first view of an Illinois Prairie is Sublime, I may almost say awfully Grand, as a person needs a compass to keep his course—but the more I travel over them the better I like them. There is a great variety of Flowers now on the Praries, but they tell me in a month from this time they will be much prettyer.

Morris Sleight, letter to his wife, 1834

Foggy morning along the Kankakee River, Kankakee River State Park

PAGE 82: Setting sun radiating through an autumn forest in Linne Woods, Cook County Forest Preserve

PAGE 83: Forest floor covered with snow in Paw Paw Woods Nature Preserve, Cook County Forest Preserve

Early autumn morning, Kankakee River State Park

Fall color of suma[...]
Indiana Dun[...]
National Lakesho[...]

Jason Linds[...]

Forest floor carpeted with ferns, Indiana Dunes National Lakeshore

Jason Lindsey

Bluebells in early bloom, Messenger Woods

Bluebells in peak bloom,
Messenger Woods

Foggy morning along the Kankakee River

Fox kit at den, Lake County

Jason Lindsey

A great blue heron, great egret, cormorant rookery on the Fox River near Tower Lakes

Jason Lindsey

I often felt sorry, … at my utter inability to fully convey to the mind of the reader the beauties of the scene in such language that might, re-produce a correct picture before the minds of my readers. I hope, however, that they may be able to so draw upon their imagination that they may fully realise the grandeur of the scenery on the banks of the Fox River.…

J. B. Loudon, *A Tour Through Canada and the United States of America*, 1878

Sunrise over the mouth of the Dead River at Lake Michigan, Illinois Beach State Park

Jason Lindsey

PAGE 94: A bullfrog surrounded by duckweed, Volo Bog State Natural Area

Robert Shaw

PAGE 95: Golden tamarack trees, Volo Bog State Natural Area

Robert Shaw

Blowing drifts at Goose Lake Prairie State Natural Area

Robert Shaw

Shooting stars, hoary
puccoon, wood
betony, and bird's-foot
violet in bloom,
Chiwaukee Prairie

Robert Shaw

Robert Shaw

Flowers again in untold numbers, were covering the prairies. and here are many . . . flowers growing wild, as blue bells, flox, bouncing bet, sweet william, roses, cocoris, beliotrope, aster, &c., beside wild flowers as fringed gentean, solidago, orchis, yellow golden rod, scarlet lilly, wild indigo, superb pink moccasin flower, and scarlet lobelia. There were many I had never seen—among them was a species of teazle, having a tall stem, purple head, surrounded by a fringe of long pink leaves—I called it the Indian fairy, for as its dark head bobbed about, and its pink mantle flowed around it, it looked like a tiny Indian. In fact, flowers

'rich as morning sunrise hue,

And gorgeous as the gemmed midnight,'

were smiling and blooming in every direction.

Eliza R. Steele, *A Summer Journey in the West*, 1840

Sumac and white birch, Indiana Dunes National Lakeshore

Maple leaves cover
the forest floor at
Ryerson Woods
Conservation Area

Sand coreopsis and downy phlox in full bloom, Illinois Beach State Park

Robert Shaw

Indian paintbrush, sand coreopsis, and downy phlox in bloom, Illinois Beach State Park

Robert Shaw

Rough blazing star, The Nature Conservancy's Indian Boundary Prairie

Jason Lindsey

PAGES 104–105:
Canada geese, Illinois
Beach State Park

Jason Lindsey

LEFT: Partridge pea
and flowering spurge
blooming at
Gensburg-Markham
Prairie

Robert Shaw

Mt. Baldy at sunrise, Indiana Dunes National Lakeshore

Robert Shaw

Jason Lindsey

Those dunes are to the Midwest what the Grand Canyon is to Arizona and the Yosemite to California. They constitute a signature of time and eternity; once lost, the loss would be irrevocable.

Carl Sandburg, letter to Senator Paul H. Douglas, 1958

A floating bullfro[g]
Volo Bog Sta[te]
Natural Are[a]

Robert Sha[w]

Water lilies cover
Lake Defiance in late
afternoon, Moraine
Hills State Park

Robert Shaw

Gulls flying over Lake Michigan at North Avenue Beach, Chicago

Jason Lindsey

Fall reflections, Kankakee River State Park

Summer dawn mist, spiderweb, and prairie grasses, Grant Creek Prairie Nature Preserve

Jason Lindsey

Jason Lindsey

The great object of our expedition, Mount Joliet, was two miles distant from this place. We had to visit it, and perform the journey back to Chicago, forty miles, before night. The mount is only sixty feet high; yet it commands a view which I shall not attempt to describe, either in its vastness, or its soft beauty. The very spirit of tranquillity resides in this paradisy scene. The next painter who would worthily illustrate Milton's Morning Hymn, should come and paint what he sees from Mount Joliet, on a dewy summer's morning, when a few light clouds are gently sailing in the sky, and their shadows traversing the prairie. I thought I had never seen green levels till now; and only among mountains had I before known the beauty of wandering showers.

Harriet Martineau, *The Prairies and Joliet*, 1836

View of downtown from the Field Museum

Robert Shaw

A little while ago ... The wilderness stood here, and the child of the forest thought of it as a prepared abiding place for himself and his people for ever. The red man has gone; the wild woods have vanished; and these structures, and vehicles, and busy crowds, have come into their places....

Edwin Hubbell Chapin, *Humanity in the City*, 1854

Morning fog rising from a pond, Illinois Beach State Park

EPILOGUE

Nature can live without people, but people cannot live without nature. Wild places are vital to both our physical and our emotional health. Parks and preserves clean the air, purify our water, manage floodwater, and provide many other life-sustaining benefits we often take for granted. Nature is also a fountain of life, housing the biological diversity that makes this planet interesting, even unique. And nature offers renewal, a sanctuary for nerve-shaken over-civilized people who find that wildness enriches and restores. How much poorer, how much duller would our lives and the lives of our children be if we never heard the call of a meadowlark, never took shade beneath the majesty of a spreading oak, never beheld the beauty of a monarch butterfly, never smelled the sweet scent of lady tresses orchids, never felt the softness of milkweed seeds.

While the quality of our lives rests with nature, it is also true that preservation of nature rests with us. As beautiful and vivid as the photographs in this book are, without our action, it is possible they could one day serve as a sad inventory of natural resources squandered. So please support conservation organizations such as The Nature Conservancy. Tell your public officials that you care about the preservation of biodiversity and wildlife habitat. Spend a day doing stewardship work at a preserve near your home. Plant an oak tree in your yard or prairie grasses in your garden. Most important, take a walk in the woods with your family and enjoy the beauty and solitude of the prairies, woodlands, wetlands, and streams of your Chicago Wilderness. As Edward Abbey once said, "It is not enough to fight for the land; it is even more important to enjoy it."

In this book, Robert Shaw and Jason Lindsay have offered striking images of a wildness that is still found in the midst of the millions of people who live in the Chicago area. We call these places Chicago Wilderness. An oxymoron, you say. Not at all. The Chicago area is home to a rich array of nature, perhaps the richest diversity of wilderness found in any metropolitan region in the world. From Lake Michigan to the Midewin National Tallgrass Prairie, from Indiana Dunes National Lakeshore through the vast forest preserves of the metropolitan region to Illinois Beach State Park and Chiwaukee Prairie, nature surrounds us. Chicago Wilderness is a rare and wonderful resource. Visit it. Save it. Treasure it.

Bruce W. Boyd, Director
The Nature Conservancy, Illinois chapter

The mission of The Nature Conservancy is to preserve plants, animals, and natural communities that represent the diversity of life on earth by protecting the lands and waters they need to survive. To date, the Conservancy and its members have been responsible for the protection of more than 11 million acres in the 50 states and Canada and have helped like-minded partner organizations preserve millions more in Latin America, the Caribbean, the Pacific, and Asia. The Conservancy owns more than 1,300 preserves, the largest private system of nature sanctuaries in the world. For more information, call (312) 346-8166 or visit the Conservancy's Web site at www.tnc.org.

A full moon setting at sunrise over the rookery on the Fox River near Tower Lakes

Robert Shaw

CHICAGO WILDERNESS STATEMENT

A rare and wondrous treasure is found in the woodlands, prairies, wetlands, and waters of the Chicago Wilderness. Harbored in 200,000 acres of county forest preserves, state parks, federal lands, and private conservation holdings is a globally significant concentration of natural biological wealth. Protecting and restoring this treasure is the mission of the Chicago Region Biodiversity Council, a coalition of more than a hundred agencies, organizations, and institutions that have pledged to work together to foster a sustainable relationship between society and nature in the Chicago region.

Jason Lindsey

Chicago Wilderness stretches from Chiwaukee Prairie in southeastern Wisconsin through northeastern Illinois to Midewin National Tallgrass Prairie and Indiana Dunes National Lakeshore in the south and east. This area includes some of the last, best remaining examples of the natural communities that once covered the Midwest and is a rich and wonderful resource that dramatically increases the quality of life for all those who live in the Chicago region.

Although a tremendous asset, our natural landscapes are in serious decline. Through unplanned and poorly planned development, invasion of aggressive, non-native species, and disruption of natural processes such as fire and habitat corridors, Chicago Wilderness is under siege. We have lost almost 90 percent of our wetlands, 80 percent of our forests, and more than 99 percent of our tallgrass prairie ecosystems. The member organizations of Chicago Wilderness realize that today we determine the legacy we will leave. Will these precious landscapes be here for our children? For their children? Will future generations know the wonder of prairie flowers and woodland birds or will they simply wonder how these treasures disappeared?

Robert Shaw

The lands of Chicago Wilderness need our help to survive and flourish. Fortunately, there are more than 5,000 dedicated volunteers working to preserve Chicago Wilderness, the largest volunteer army of its kind anywhere in the world. And the Chicago Region Biodiversity Council has developed the Biodiversity Recovery Plan, a comprehensive blueprint for the protection and restoration of Chicago Wilderness.

Nature gives us so much—recreation . . . lifesaving medicines . . . flood prevention . . . a home for wildlife. You are invited to join the thousands of people who are giving back—healing the earth for a healthier environment, for the beauty of nature, and for future generations. To learn more about Chicago Wilderness, call any member organization or (708) 485-0263, extension 396. Or visit the Chicago Wilderness Web site at www.chicagowilderness.org for events and volunteer opportunities.

CHICAGO WILDERNESS MEMBER ORGANIZATIONS

Bird Conservation Network
(847) 864-6393

Brookfield Zoo
www.brookfieldzoo.org
(708) 485-0263

Butterfield Creek Steering Committee
(708) 798-2300

Calumet Ecological Park Association
www.lincolnnet.net/cepa
(708) 841-0174

Calumet Environmental Resource Center
www.csu.edu/cerc
(773) 995-2964

Campaign for Sensible Growth
csg@metroplanning.org
(312) 922-5616

Campton Historic Agricultural Lands, Inc.
(630) 584-8485

Canal Corridor Association
www.canalcor.org
(312) 427-3688

Cary Park District
(847) 639-6100

Center for Neighborhood Technology
www.cnt.org
(773) 278-4800

Chicago Academy of Sciences
www.chias.org
(773) 549-0606

Chicago Audubon Society
www.audubon.org/chapter/il/chicago
(773) 539-6793

Chicago Botanic Garden
www.chicago-botanic.org
(847) 835-5440

Chicago Ornithological Society
(630) 985-2956

Chicago Park District
www.chicagoparkdistrict.com
(312) 747-2200

Chicagoland Bird Observatory
(630) 243-6394

Citizens for Conservation
www.chicagotribune.com/link/cfc
(847) 382-7283

City of Chicago, Department of Environment
www.ci.chi.il.us/WorksMart/Environment
(312) 744-7606

College of DuPage
www.cod.edu
(630) 942-2010

The Conservation Foundation
www.conservationfoun.org
(630) 682-3505

The Conservation Fund
www.conservationfund.org
(312) 913-9065

Conservation Research Institute
(630) 832-8322

Crystal Lake Park District
(815) 455-1763

DePaul University, Environmental Science Program
www.depaul.edu/~envirsci/
(773) 325-7447

Downers Grove Park District
www.dgparks.org
(630) 963-1300

Ducks Unlimited — Great Lakes/Atlantic Regional Office
www.ducks.org
(734) 623-2000

DuPage Audubon Society
(847) 299-7882

Emily Oaks Nature Center — Skokie Park District
(847) 677-7001

Environmental Law and Policy Center of the Midwest
www.elpc.org
(312) 759-3707

The Field Museum
www.fmnh.org
(312) 922-9410

Forest Preserve District of Cook County
(708) 366-9420

Forest Preserve District of DuPage County
www.dupageforest.com
(630) 790-4900

Forest Preserve District of Kane County
www.co.kane.il.us/forest
(630) 232-5980

Forest Preserve District of Will County
www.fpdwc.org
(815) 727-8700

Fox Valley Land Foundation
(847) 697-7764

Friends of the Chicago River
www.chicagoriver.org
(312) 939-0490

Friends of the Parks
www.fotp.org
(312) 857-2757

Friends of Ryerson Woods
www.village.lincolnshire.il.us/vill_org/ryerson.html
(847) 948-7750

Garfield Park Conservatory Alliance
www.garfield-conservatory.org
(773) 638-1766

Geneva Park District
www.genevaparks.org
(630) 262-8244

Glenview Prairie Preservation Project
www.glenviewprairie.org
(847) 291-7434

The Grove National Historic Landmark
(847) 299-6096

Hammond Environmental Education Center
(219) 933-6075

Illinois Audubon Society
www.illinoisaudubon.org
(217) 446-5085

Illinois Audubon Society, Fort Dearborn Chapter
(847) 475-3895

Illinois Department of Natural Resources
dnr.state.il.us
(217) 782-6302

Illinois-Indiana Sea Grant College Program
ag.ansc.purdue.edu/il-in-sg
(765) 494-3573

Illinois Natural History Survey
www.inhs.uiuc.edu
(217) 333-6880

Illinois Nature Preserves Commission
dnr.state.il.us/inpc
(217) 785-8686

Indiana Department of Natural Resources
www.state.in.us/dnr
(317) 232-4052

Indiana Dunes Environmental Learning Center
www.nps.gov/indu/learning
(219) 395-9555

Indiana University Northwest, Department of Biology
(219) 980-7760

Irons Oaks Environmental Learning Center
(708) 481-2330

Jurica Nature Museum
(630) 829-6546

Kane-DuPage Soil & Water Conservation District
www.inil.com/users/kdswcd
(630) 584-7961

Lake County Forest Preserves
www.co.lake.il.us/forest
(847) 367-6640

Lake County Stormwater Management Commission
(847) 918-5260

Lake Forest Open Lands Association
www.lfola.org
(847) 234-3880

Lake Michigan Federation
www.lakemichigan.org
(312) 939-0838

Liberty Prairie Conservancy
www.libertyprairie.org
(847) 548-5989

Lincoln Park Zoo
www.lpzoo.com
(312) 742-2000

Long Grove Park District
(847) 438-4743

Loyola University, College of Arts and Sciences
(773) 508-3500

Max McGraw Wildlife Foundation
(847) 741-8000

McHenry County Conservation District
(815) 678-4431

Metropolitan Water Reclamation District of Greater Chicago
www.mwrdgc.dst.il.us
(312) 751-6634

Morton Arboretum
www.mortonarb.org
(630) 968-0074

National Audubon Society
www.audubon.org
(847) 965-1150

The Nature Conservancy
www.tnc.org
(312) 346-8166

NiSource Environmental Challenge Fund
(219) 647-5262

North Cook County Soil & Water Conservation District
(847) 468-0071

Northbrook Park Districk
(847) 291-2960

Northeastern Illinois University
www.neiu.edu
(773) 583-4050

Northeastern Illinois Planning Commission
www.nipc.cog.il.us
(312) 454-0400

Northwest Indiana Forum Foundation, Inc.
www.nwiforum.org
(219) 763-6303

Northwestern Indiana Regional Planning Commission
www.nirpc.org
(219) 763-6060

Oakbrook Terrace Park District
www.obtpd.org
(630) 941-8747

Openlands Project
www.openlands.org
(312) 427-4256

Palos-Orland Conservation Committee
(708) 448-4242

Palos Park Tree Foundation
(708) 448-2700

Park District of Highland Park
(847) 681-2189

Prairie Woods Audubon Society
(847) 952-5821

River Forest Park District
(708) 366-6660

Save the Dunes Conservation Fund
www.savedunes.org
(219) 879-3564

Save the Prairie Society
www.applicom.com/sps
(708) 865-8736

Schaumburg Park District — Spring Valley Nature Sanctuary
www.schaumburgparkdistrict.com
(847) 985-2100

John G. Shedd Aquarium
www.sheddnet.org
(312) 939-2438

Shirley Heinze Environmental Fund
www.savedunes.org/html/shef.html
(219) 879-4725

Sierra Club, Illinois Chapter
www.sierraclub.org
(312) 251-1680

St. Charles Park District
www.st-charlesparks.org
(630) 513-3338

Sustain, The Environmental Information Group
(312) 951-8999

Thorn Creek Audubon Society
(708) 799-0249

The Trust for Public Land
www.tpl.org
(312) 427-1979

Town Square Condominium Assocation
(847) 985-8595

Urban Resources Partnership
(312) 353-2473

US Army Corps of Engineers, Chicago District
(312) 353-6400

US Department of Energy, Argonne National Laboratory
www.anl.gov
(630) 252-5562

US Department of Energy, Fermi National Accelerator Laboratory
www.fnal.gov
(630) 840-3351

US Environmental Protection Agency, Region 5
www.epa.gov/region5
(800) 621-8431

US EPA Great Lakes National Program Office
www.epa.gov/grtlakes
(800) 621-8431

USDA Forest Service
www.fs.fed.us
(847) 866-9311

USDA Natural Resources Conservation Service
www.il.nrcs.usda.gov
(630) 505-7808

USDI Fish & Wildlife Service
www.fws.gov
(847) 381-2253

USDI National Park Service
www.nps.gov
(402) 221-3471

Village of Riverside
(708) 447-2700

The Wetlands Initiative
www.wetlands-initiative.org
(312) 922-0777

Wild Ones Natural Landscapers, Ltd.
www.for-wild.org
(312) 845-5116

Members as of May 2000

Morning light on rattlesnake master and spiderweb, The Nature Conservancy's Biesecker Prairie, Indiana

Jason Lindsey

Wood sculpture at Indiana Dunes State Park   Robert Shaw

BIBLIOGRAPHY

Algren, Nelson. *Chicago: City on the Make* (New York: Doubleday, 1951).

Angle, Paul M., editor. *Prairie State—Impressions of Illinois 1673–1967 by Travelers and Other Observers* (Chicago: University of Chicago Press, 1968).

Chapin, Edwin Hubbell. *Humanity in the City* (New York: Arno Press, 1974).

Chapin, Louella. *Round About Chicago* (Chicago: Unity Publishing Company, 1907).

Fuller, Sarah Margaret. *Summer on the Lakes, 1843* (Urbana: University of Illinois Press, 1991).

Steele, Eliza R. *A Summer Journey in the West* (New York: J. S. Taylor, 1841).

Waldron, Larry. *The Indiana Dunes* (Eastern National, 1998).

Clouds reflecting in the Dead River, Illinois Beach State Park

Jason Lindsey

PHOTOGRAPHIC INFORMATION

Robert Shaw's Images

These images were created on three formats. Nearly all landscapes were photographed with a Sinar 4 x 5 view camera using six Nikkor lenses. I also used two Pentax 6 x 7 cameras with seven Pentax lenses in harsh winter conditions. The wildlife photography and close-ups were made using Nikon cameras and optics. Two Nikon F4s and an F5 camera were used with several Nikkor lenses, ranging from 24mm to 500mm, and one Nikkor 1x teleconverter.

When photographing landscapes, exposures were calculated with a Minolta spotmeter. When working with the Nikon F4 and F5, I always used the camera's spotmeter.

Two types of filtration were used. B+W Kaesemann and Top polarization filters, and B+W 81B filters were used when necessary with the larger formats. A Nikon 81A filter was used occasionally with the Nikkor tele-photo lenses.

All photographs were made on Gitzo tripods using a Wimberley Design head and a Studioball ballhead for 35mm work and a Bogen pan-tilt head for landscapes. All photographs were made with Fuji transparency films.

Jason Lindsey's Images

These images were created using a Nikon F5 and a N90s with several Nikkor lenses, ranging from 28mm to 300mm, and one Nikkor 2x teleconverter. Exposures were calculated with the camera's spotmeter. A Nikon polarization filter, a Nikon 81A filter, and Singh-Ray graduated neutral density filters were occasionally used. All photographs were made on Gitzo tripods using a Arca-Swiss ballhead. Fuji Velvi and Provia along with some Kodak E100s transparency films were used.

Three Important Notes

The photographs in this book were taken within 55 miles of downtown Chicago.

The animals and plants pictured in this book are all living in the wild.

No manipulation or alteration was made to any photograph in this book.

To order prints, notecards, calendars, and stock photography, contact:

Robert Shaw
Wild Perceptions
P.O. Box 590
Heyworth, IL 61745
(309) 473-2990
mail@wildperceptions.com
www.wildperceptions.com

Jason Lindsey
(217) 637-0069
jason@perceptivevisions.com
www.perceptivevisions.com

Jason Lindsey (left), Robert Shaw (right)   David Hessel

Robert and Jason after photographing at   Tom Holmes
Goose Lake Prairie on a -10° afternoon

Jason Lindsey photographing the   Robert Shaw
blowing sands on Mt. Baldy

VISITOR'S GUIDE

This guide is a starting point for exploring the natural wonders of the Chicago area. It is not intended to be a complete guide but rather an introduction to the variety of natural habitats featured in this book. These parks all have good public access. We hope you enjoy visiting them and become inspired to do your part in protecting these natural wonders. Please explore them responsibly, and remember, "Take only pictures, leave only footprints."

Illinois Beach State Park

Explore the only remaining natural coastline of Lake Michigan in Illinois. This is one of the best locations in Illinois to see the spring and fall migrations of hawks.

300 Lakefront Drive
Zion, IL 60099
(847) 662-4828

Indiana Dunes National Lakeshore

Hike to the top of Mt. Baldy, a 190-foot sand dune, for the most dramatic view of Lake Michigan in the Chicago region. Also a great place to see biodiversity, Indiana Dunes is ranked seventh among national parks in native plant diversity.

1100 North Mineral Springs Road
Porter, Indiana 46304
(219) 926-7561

Indiana Dunes State Park

This park is located within the National Lakeshore. Trail 9 through the Dunes Nature Preserve offers a spectacular vista of Lake Michigan and the Chicago skyline beyond.

1600 N. 25E
Chesterton, Indiana 46304
(219) 926-1952

Goose Lake Prairie State Natural Area

Take a hike on trails that wind through native prairie grasses and experience the Illinois tall-grass prairie as pioneer settlers once did.

5010 N. Jugtown Road
Morris, IL 60450
(815) 942-2899

Camp Sagawau

Explore Cook County's only canyon and learn about its unique plant communities and cultural history. To preserve the fragile ecosystem of the canyon, you must call for reservations and tour with a naturalist.

1255 W. 111th Street
Lemont, IL 60439
(630) 257-2045

Messenger Woods

A late April or early May hike will reveal the most spectacular display of woodland wildflowers in the state of Illinois.

Messenger Woods is located on Bruce Road, north of Route 6 (Southwest Highway) and east of Cedar Road, in rural Lockport.
Will County Forest Preserve District Office
P.O. Box 1069
Joliet IL 60434
(815) 727-8700

Wolf Road Prairie

This Cook County Forest Preserve is considered one of the best black-soil prairie ecosystems east of the Mississippi River. The prairie is most spectacular during the summer months.

31st Street and Wolf Road
Westchester, IL 60153
(708) 771-1330

Chain O'Lakes State Park

An early morning hike along the Fox River in late spring or early summer may provide a glimpse of courting sandhill cranes. They have now returned to Lake County nesting sites.

8916 Wilmot Road
Spring Grove, IL 60081
(847) 587-5512

Kankakee River State Park

A hike during any season along Rock Creek Canyon provides some of the most dramatic views in the state of Illinois. The trail along the Kankakee River is great for a family bike ride.

From Bourbonnais, the state park is located 7 miles west on Rte. 102.
P.O. Box 37
Bourbonnais, IL 60914
(815) 933-1383

Des Plaines Fish and Wildlife Area/ Grant Creek Prairie

Beginning in summer and continuing into fall, Grant Creek Prairie is an ever-changing display of color and diversity.

24621 N. River Road
Wilmington, IL 60481
(815) 423-5326

Volo Bog

This is one of the most fascinating natural areas in Illinois. A wooden walkway leads visitors over the bog and provides a glimpse of tamrac trees growing on a floating mat of peat.

28478 W. Brandenburg Road
Ingleside, IL 60041
(815) 344-1294

Ryerson Woods

This enchanting old-growth woodland has 6 miles of trails to explore, with one trail following the Des Plaines River. This park is beautiful in every month of the year.

21950 N. Riverwoods Road
Deerfield, IL 60015
(847) 948-7750

Moraine Hills State Park

Bring your binoculars along for a birding adventure as you hike the boardwalk through a wetland and along waterlily-covered Defiance Lake.

914 S. River Road
McHenry, IL 60050
(815) 385-1624

Pilcher Park

If you cannot wait for spring, a hike in late March reveals its earliest signs with the sighting of skunk cabbage. Later in the spring, a sea of green and yellow can be found with the blooming of marsh marigold among the skunk cabbage.

Joliet Park District
3000 W. Jefferson Street
Joliet, IL 60435
(815) 741-7577